Hope & Other Things

Ms Moem

Positive Press
2018

First Printing: 2018

ISBN 978-0-244-07161-5

www.msmoem.com

Dedication

For Clink, Jim, Bean & Susan,
You are my endless hope!

I love you.

Contents

70. Undefeated
71. Brimful Of Aspiration
72. Dare To Self Care
73. Out Of Our Hands
74. The Universe Got Your Back
75. Starmaker
76. Happy Memories
77. Let Love Shout Loudest

1.

1.   She Wrote A Life She Loved

She wrote a life she loved
On the leaves of many books,
Documenting all the details
So that one day she could look
Back on all that she had done
And all that she had seen;
All the people she had known,
All the places she had been.
And there upon the paper
Her treasures, line by line,
Imbued with emotion
Invoke moments in time.
So although this was a story
That only she could tell,
The ink left upon her pages said
"My word. She lived it well."

2.

2. Story Arc

There's a poem in your pocket
And a novel in your chest,
With the plot lines weaved in silver
Threaded through your thorny vest.
Your roots are well established
And your bark protects your core
But there's intrigue in your trunk;
Your rings now tell us more.
Revealing your beleaguered story
Litters lines of dog-eared leaves.
Nonchalant nomads nimble
On the nuances of the breeze.

3.

3. You Deserve Kindness

You deserve kindness. I mean it. It's true.
Yes, you deserve kindness, from me, and from you.
Be kind to yourself when you see your reflection.
There's only one you, and no such thing as perfection.
Beware the inner critic who lives in your mind
And break free from its prison that holds you confined.
It might tell you you're ugly, or stupid, or worse
But frankly, its outlook is simply perverse.
So be kind to yourself, and to others around;
Lift yourself up instead of putting yourself down.
You're magnificent as you are, if you don't know it yet
And you do deserve kindness. Please don't ever forget.

4.

4. Memories Are Funny Things

Memories are funny things.
You hear your favourite singer sing
And all at once, that voice is stored,
Recognizable evermore.

You visit towns, you see the sights,
You feel the heat, you see the light
And that becomes a picture, saved;
A snapshot of a happy day.

And all you ever need to do
Is think about that perfect view
And all at once, you're there once more,
Seeing it as you previously saw.

A scent or sound can do the same.
A hint, and whoosh, you're back again.
You're in the room, you're with the guy,
No matter how much time's passed by.

And if you listen close enough
The voices of the ones you love
Will stay inside your clever mind
For you to recall, anytime!

So soak up life and all it brings
Cos memories are funny things.
They're weaved from all you see or do.
Make them good. It's up to you.

5.

5. Carry On

We've cried an endless river.
Our hope stores all but drained.
Your echoes are fading quickly;
Intensifying our pain.
Your fingerprints all washed away.
We pack away your clothes.
Your room lays bare and empty.
Your door permanently closed.
You've slipped into another world;
A place we cannot be.
Time can no longer touch you
And sadly, nor can we.
And so the dark turns into night,
The sun all set and gone.
Yet though our tears have blurred our sight
Your memory spurs us on.

6.

6. Balloons

I saw balloons float past me,
Saw them sail into the sky.
I assumed that those who lost them
Would have tears in their eyes.
But I found them; they were smiling
and were keen to let me know
that those balloons were full of troubles
so they'd simply let them go.

7.

7. Being Alone

There is comfort in being alone.
Especially when safely at home,
With a nice cup of tea,
Just my own thoughts and me,
Yes, there's comfort in being alone.
There's a lesson in being alone.
In that space, many great minds have grown.
You are you, no-one else,
Just be true to yourself.
There's a lesson in being alone.

8.

8. Insight

I'm not surprised you can't set sight
On how your life should be
Because our lives are largely shaped
By forces we can't see.

9.

9. Count All The Ways You're Beautiful

Count all the ways you're beautiful;
Your soul and your spirit,
Your brilliant body
And all the wonder within it.
Your heart full of love,
Your mind full of care,
Your eyes full of awe,
Your lungs full of air.
Your chest full of pride,
Your muscles full of strength,
Your brain full of questions,
Your compassion, immense.
Your hands that can comfort,
Your words that can soothe,
Your conscience that roots you
In the good, right and true.
You are a miracle,
Unique through and through.
So count the ways you're beautiful
And always be proud of you!

10.

10. Life Hacks

Listen for the positive,
The voice that talks you down.
The one who tells you that they care;
That they like you around.
And when you're standing on the ledge,
They're waiting in the wings,
Reminding you that life is full
Of hope and other things.

11.

11. Metamorphosis

I'm tired of waiting, being stuck on the verge.
Done being a caterpillar, I long to emerge
As a beautiful butterfly, flying free in the world.
It's all that I've dreamt of since I was a girl.

12.

12.   Not So Different

You don't hear music like I do. You don't feel the things that I feel.
You don't respect the same values I do, though that doesn't make them
less valid or real.
You don't choose to pursue the things that I do, you just don't see the
appeal.
You don't want the same things that I want. You've got your eye on a
different deal.

You don't believe in the same things that I do. Your religion and beliefs
are all yours.
You don't question things in the way that I do. You don't just think
you're right, you're sure.
You don't see things in their simplicity, you are convinced there is
always more.
You don't think there is validity in any other way. You don't even falter
or pause.

You don't wear the clothes that I wear. You don't have the same colour
eyes or skin.
You are different to me in many ways, from what's outside, to what's
within.
We are individualized at birth, at the moment we are given our name
But we should stop focusing on our differences, and look at what
makes us the same.

We'll push aside all barriers
and break down all walls.
This is a free world
and there is room for us all.

13.

13. Epilogue

One day they'll write our epilogue
and I want it to say
that this pair stuck together
for all of their days.
They loved one another;
they made a great team,
they shared hopes and goals
and went after their dreams.
They weathered the storms,
made hay in the sun,
saw family and friends
and always had fun.
But above all I hope
that if it came to it,
if asked to repeat time
we'd be happy to do it.

14.

14. Friendship Matters

A friend is pleased to see you.
Friendship is based on care.
A friend won't leave you high & dry.
A true friend's always there.

15.

15. Does Size Matter?

"I'm small and insignificant,"
he said with sorry sighs,
and mused on the magnificence
of space, beyond our skies.
He sought out stars and planets
seeking salience and signs
of potential explanations
to our existence and design.
At the edges of the universe
he looked back and realised
that the measure of significance
was never based on size.

16.

16.   Back To Being Human

Let's get back to being human
as we lost it some way back.
We devolved to war and warriors;
let's regain the human track.

Let's get back to being human.
It's who we're meant to be.
It's true that we are complex
but we can live in harmony.

Let's get back to being human.
What does that mean to you?
Is it wrapped up in your words or thoughts
and all the things you do?

Let's get back to being human.
I really feel we should
as what it means to be human
is coursing through our blood.

17.

17.   Wild One

And they say she's a wild one,
She knows her own mind.
She flits on the breeze,
Colours outside the lines.
Because they can't place her
Her world stays un-mapped
But she carries on driving
And never looks back.

18.

18.   I Am Your Star

Remember me with heartfelt smiles
(The sort that shines for miles and miles)
For while you're sad and feeling low
Nothing can change. I had to go.
But if you face the world and grin,
Keep memories safe and warm within,
Then somewhere, deep inside your heart
You'll almost feel we're not apart.
We see stars shining in the sky
Forgetting they have long since died.
So, see that light and feel it too.
I am your star. I shone for you.

19.

19. Love Them Harder

Whether son or daughter,
Mother of father,
Cherish your people.
Love them harder.

20.

20. Tenses

Remember how we used to be
Before our lives were one.
You were you, and I was me;
Just bumbling along.
Now I is us and also we,
We found where we belong.

Imagine how our future lies
And what might be in store.
We'll face whatever, side by side;
That's what our team is for.
And you'll still give me butterflies
Just like you did before.

Our present is a gift to live
With days of purest pleasure.
Each can take and also give
In mostly equal measure.
In short, you're who I should be with,
To share this life forever.

21.

21. Wounded

To lose someone you love
Is to tear your world apart.
You step, when moving forward,
On the pieces of your heart.
You try to patch your injuries
To pull yourself together
But underneath your bandages
The cuts stay fresh forever.

22.

22. Moving Forward

Moving forward. Onward. Up.
Choose the way you see your cup.
Half depleted? Semi-full?
Grab the horns. Steer that bull.

23.

23. Designed For Life

Be your own inspiration,
When times seem bleak or tough,
When you're looking for motivation
Or proof that you are enough.
You trust your individual components;
Your eyes, your fingers, your brain.
Those parts do what they're meant to do.
The sum and total are the same!
Know there is strength inside you.
Know with each beat of your heart
That you can do what you are meant to do;
All you have to do is start.

24.

24. Wolves In Their Eyes

Sometimes we get a glimpse of soul
in things we've seen or heard.
Others can reveal themselves
without ever saying a word.
Some pretend to be sheep
when they're really wolves in disguise
and you see nothing but your reflection
as you look into their cold, dead eyes.

25.

25. Where I'll Always Be

I could never hope to find
Someone who fits me better.
I swear I made a wish and it
Was answered to the letter.
I hope that you feel just the same.
I think I know you do.
I swear I had a dream one night
And now it's coming true.
You're all I ever wanted
And you're all I ever will.
My love in its happy place
And growing greater still,
As every day I spend with you
I see more that I like.
You could make the greyest day
Feel sunny, warm and bright.
You're such a special person
And you mean the world to me.
So any time or place you are,
That's where I'll always be.

26.

26. Home

This is our base, our favourite place
our beginning and end to each day.
It's our triumph and glory, that these walls tell stories
as they soak up all we do and say.
This is our space. Each corner is laced
with items we've chosen with care.
From sweet scented candles, to fixtures & handles
the atmosphere's just right to share.
So near or so far, wherever we are,
no matter where we choose to roam,
we live and we learn, but we always return;
This the place we call home.

27.

27. Little Dancer

That clumsy little dancer
Who twirls about your hall,
May one day lose their sparkle
And their will to twirl at all.
So smile when you see it;
Drink those moments in
Before society extinguishes
The spark that burns within.

28.

28.   A Note To Creatives

Suffering from creative block?
Please do not despair.
Like many things, it can be coaxed
With love and tender care.
First, discard the worry
And let your mind be clear.
Leave room for inspiration.
Make space for fresh ideas.
Next, reignite your senses;
Seek out something new.
Look from different angles
Or do things you rarely do.
Research a passion project.
Follow links that inspire.
Nurture all glowing embers
So those sparks can take fire.
Banish fear and pressure,
Let your block melt away.
Then step into the arena
And live to create another day.

29.

29. Trading Grains

They packaged up the gift of time
And presented it in glass.
A disclaimer on the bottom said;
temporary, this will pass.

It sat upon so many shelves
In just the perfect spot.
Though glanced upon a time or two
It appeared not to change a lot.

It stood there morning, night & noon;
A vessel of promise & plenty.
Others came to share the dune
And stayed 'til it was empty.

They traded grains for memories,
For moments mad and wild.
They took some time to make some more
To pass on to their child.

Each mass of sand will drain away
And not one grain will linger.
Just make sure you enjoy your time
Before it slips through your fingers.

30.

30. Hopes & Dreams

Hope is optimistic.
Hope is host to dreams.
Hope was there and brought us here
And pushed us in between.
But they don't want us dreaming
For fear we will not wake.
Regret will leave us screaming
For those dreams weren't theirs to take.
So hold onto your hopefulness.
Don't let the dream slayers win,
As once they stop you dreaming
That's when the nightmare begins.

31.

31.   Here's To Right Now

You're surrounded by your loved ones
And all are wishing you well
As you create a brand new chapter
In the story that's yours to tell.

We talk about the memories
You have yet to make together
And the moments you've already shared
To be carried with you forever.

But take the time to live today
As your marriage begins.
Look around and soak it up;
the moment we are in.

For this is where the magic starts
When you both say your vows.
You pledge to spend your lives as one
Because of the love you feel now.

So yes, here's to a future that is bright and warm and clear
But more than that, here's to right now, and what it means to be here.

32.

32. Irresistible

There's been an undeniable truth
Since before we even existed;
Nothing ever stays the same.
Change cannot be resisted.

33.

33. Locked Away

She posts pictures of the most amazing life.
The day she became a wife
she wore crystal shoes,
that her loving sister and proud mama helped her choose.
They had spent a glorious day trawling
luxury bridal boutiques,
then gone to a fancy cafe for a lunch time treat.
The afternoon had seen her swathed in silk;
cream, not white because the sales assistant
said her beautiful milky complexion
would be better complimented that way.
So she'd been primped and preened for her perfect day.

She was a stunning bride.

Then babies arrived. Chubby bundles of perfection
who took their beauty from their mother.
And a helpful husband who made sure they still
spent quality time with each other.

The date night surprises,
and breakfast in bed.
Her life seems like a mills and boon romance
Begging to be read.

She is doing everything right.
A healthy balance of nights out with
her many chums,
and she's a divine example of a perfect wife
a perfect mum
And everyone holds the impression that she's doing more than ok.
Because she shows no trace of her depression. She locks that away.

34.

34. Remember

Remember when your separate lives were all there was to know,
Before the spark, the first connect, the love that came to grow.
Remember how you met and how it changed it your lives forever,
As from then on, your lives entwined and you did things together.
Remember what you did back then and how it made you feel;
A sneaky touch, the cheeky looks, the pure raw sex appeal.
Remember who was first to move and how they made it clear
Nothing to prove, when all was new, the path that led you here.
Remember where it started and look how far you've come.
Remember all the words you said and all that you have done.
Remember where you're going and how it came to start
And remember that you choose the ones who occupy your heart.

35.

35. Friends

From the day life starts until it ends
We have the chance to make lots of friends.
They're dotted all about life's line,
To chatter to, to pass the time.
To show support, to be a mate,
To make sure that you celebrate
The milestones you have reached and passed;
To hold your hand as you breathe your last.
There are friends who you'd do anything for
Who never ask for anything more
Than companionship and fun and laughter;
No need to wonder what they're after.
They're there to listen when you're in need.
They offer advice and you take heed
Because you know their intentions are good
And they'd always help you if they could.
Then there are friends who take, take, take
And though, not bad, they seem to make
A mountain of the smallest matters;
Those friendships seem to end in tatters.
The ones who, when your problems mount,
Just disappear, and you can't count
On them at all, not necessarily because they're mean
But rather because it's just the way they've always been.

Spending time with friends is a great thing to do.
You find them near, you find them far.
You're not responsible for how others are
But what kind of friend are you?

36.

36. Solidarity

What happened to solidarity? It's become a harsh world
With so much division, especially amongst girls.
You profess your disdain with a sneer or a nudge
And really, we're all sisters, and we have no right to judge.
So what if her skirt's short? So what if she's fat?
So what if she's happy to be acting like that?
So what if she's different? So what if she's quiet?
So what if she prescribes to her own unique diet?
You don't see a toddler looking forlornly in the mirror
Thinking 'look at my tummy, how I wish I were thinner.'
She doesn't pass judgement nor compare herself to others
And she sees nothing but love when she looks at her mother.
Then I don't know what happens, I think it's at school
But you suddenly become quite aware you're not cool.
You wish you could change, and look like someone else
And suddenly you're no longer in awe of yourself.
You're weighing yourself up, comparing your thighs;
You think you want different hair, perhaps different eyes.
You wish you went in where your body goes out.
Your whole sense of being is battered with doubt.
I wish we could pinpoint when exactly this begins,
Where it becomes less about self-evolution and more about fitting in.
As long as you're hurting no-one, then tell me, where's the harm?
We're all unique beings with our own certain charm.
So be the best you, encourage others to do the same
And don't say anything mean that might cause another pain.
You don't need to voice your criticisms, so I would urge you to think
twice.
Simply try to be kind, and just say something nice.
The most beautiful people are those with the kindest hearts
And they know there is no reason to pull other people apart.

37.

37. Family Matters

You could gather a million treasures.
You could search from coast to coast.
The most valuable thing you'll find
Is that family matters most.

38.

38. The Lost Christmas

Have you heard of the lost Christmas?
It's not mentioned a lot.
But in depths of a brutal winter
One year Santa forgot!
He'd been out with the lads
And he'd had too much gin.
It meant he missed work
Because alas, he slept in.

Mrs Claus was no use.
In fact she was as bad.
She'd been acting the barmaid;
Entertaining the lads.
She made the boys roar with a flash of her thighs
And did something unspeakable with two hot fresh mince pies!

Anyway, the upshot;
It destroyed all their plans
And families sat baffled, with their heads in their hands.
There were children sat sobbing
And Mums shaking their fists.
Dads trying to gain web access
To the fabled naughty list.

They checked on Santa's twitter and his facebook page too.
All they found was a selfie from the Lapland Christmas Do.
He'd not updated his status to say he was primed
And Norad simply said "There's no movement at this time".

There was no sign of Rudolph
And no word from the elves
So reluctantly the parents

Took the jobs on themselves.

There was no time to waste,
They could moan about it later.
They set about finding presents
And wrapping them in paper.
Mum persuaded Dad to slip on a red suit
Then sent him on his way, to his entrance via the roof.
He got halfway up the drainpipe, but couldn't go any higher
Realising his route was blocked by the fancy electric fire.

He clambered down defeated, knowing his wife would send him back
When he simply wanted to get to the point, and empty his special sack.
At this point it was getting late, and the day looked to be lost
But he was determined to give his kids Christmas, and he would do it at
any cost.

So he hopped onto the landline, you know the thing that no-one uses,
And when Santa finally answered, Dad was taking no excuses.
He said he better get here or if he didn't there would be trouble
And he demanded that as compensation, the amount of presents should
now be double.
He didn't give him a chance to say that this would not occur
As Mum was looking on, and frankly he was more scared of her.
So Santa apologised profusely and said that he was on his way
And he hoped he'd make it over there, before the end of Christmas day.

Eventually he made it, and the children clapped with glee.
Dad just raised his eyebrows, and gestured to where the gifts should be.
Mum said "Come on Nigel, it doesn't matter that he was late.
He's here and he's brought goodies, and I think he's pretty great.
In fact, forgive my boldness, but I really love what you do
And I've never met someone so famous, so can I get a picture with
you?"

Dad just couldn't believe it. He was raging, that's for sure.

Just hours ago this woman said she had no faith in Santa any more.
Now here she was swooning, with stars in her eyes
Over an old man with a hangover, barely legal to fly.

It all got quite messy . The police came in the end.
They weren't sure if he could press charges. Said it would depend
As there was no sign of a break-in, and St.Nick was always good to the force...
They said they'd seen all they needed, and they'd be in touch in due course.

Santa scarpered sharpish, Dad nursed his black eye.
Mum tried to console the children, said there was no need to cry.
She offered up turkey sandwiches, but no one felt like eating.
It's not Christmas when you've seen Santa give your Dad a good beating.

So no-one ever mentions it, and now you know why.
The legend of the year that Santa forgot to take to the sky.
He has never let it happen since, and just to make extra sure
He's now moved his Christmas party .... to the weekend before!

39.

39.   No-One Ever Wins A War

No-one ever wins a war.
Just take a look at history and all that came before,
no-one ever, and I mean no-one, truly ever wins a war.
How can anyone expect world changes
from the senseless murders of strangers.
Strangers to us and strangers to their killers,
yet we all bear the scars and danger dances within us.
Contempt and distrust rise triumphant from the dust.
Not a single drop of blood spilled is necessary or just.
And yet it goes on. An eye for an eye, a bomb for a bomb.
People flee from their countries and the war rages on.
And for what? What's it solving?
Stuck in a loop, a door revolving;
revolvers handed to misguided fighters
to intimidate and destroy, to decimate and incite us
to respond.
With yet more bombs.
Who started what is not the focus that matters
but endless retaliation leaves families in tatters.
Towns turn to rubble, hope turns to horror,
today turns to terror, what's left for tomorrow?
It is a hollow sort of victory
that sees those written down in history
only have their notoriety
because of the hurt they caused society.
And whilst hurt breeds fear,
fear builds walls.
Walls divide still further
and division kills us all.
And what's it for?
No-one ever wins a war.

It doesn't bring freedom, or friendship, and more
it doesn't unite communities or legitimise a cause.
No, no-one ever wins a war.

40.

40. Nature

Our fundamental origins,
Immeasurable worth.
Beautiful by default,
Born of the earth.
We abuse and destroy it
Despite it all it gives
But nature is powerful;
It surrounds us.
It lives.

41.

41.   The Wishes That Never Came True

He blew his birthday candles out.
Her penny hit the well.
They closed their eyes, and dreamed a dream
That they would a never tell.
The children pulled the wishbone.
Dandelion seeds dispersed.
Fingers crossed so hopefully;
Rituals well-rehearsed.
But no-one ever mentions,
Though successes counted are few,
The wishes made upon a star
That never did come true.

42.

42. Soul Gazing

To know a person better,
To appreciate them as a whole,
Just look into their eyes
As they're the windows to the soul.

43.

43. Mind Reader

Sometimes I like to assume that others can read minds
So when I'm standing there in front of them, saying that I'm fine,
That they'd say to me, now really, you don't have to pretend.
I can see something is bugging you. Come on, tell me, I'm your friend.
But of course they never say that as of course I never said
As I prefer to leave things simmering and multiplying in my head.

44.

44. Footprints

Wherever you walk
Your impression is left;
You leave footprints all over my soul.
You enrich my life
When once I was half
I now am most definitely whole.

Where you go I'll follow,
Today and tomorrow,
Life's journey together we'll face.
And here on this road
We'll share any load
On our way to a happier place.

45.

45. I Choose You

Life can be thought as a series of choices made;
We hope to look back and smile as our memories are replayed.
Those once in a lifetime moments aren't always quick to show
But when they do materialise, then somehow you just know.

I am happier now than I ever thought I would be;
I love the person you are and the person you make me.
We share an understanding, we share hopes and goals.
Together, united, we're two halves of one whole.

I will never take for granted that you've given me your heart
And I gently carry it with me whenever we are apart.
In return, I give you mine, to cherish and to hold.
No promise is too great to make, you're worth your weight in gold.

Promises made. Vows declared.
A dream to build. A life to share.
I'm proud to utter the words 'I do'
As it tells the world that I choose you.

46.

46. Hold My Hand Mummy

Hold my Hand, Mummy,
And show me the way,
So that I can go out
In the big world one day.
Teach me the basics,
And then let me learn.
Should I ever get stuck,
I will know where to turn.
Cheer me up, Mummy,
When I'm feeling blue.
I can always rely
On a kind word from you.
Dry my tears, Mummy,
When I'm feeling sad.
Let me know it's okay,
And I won't feel so bad.
Show me the sunshine,
And then set me free.
To be the brilliant person,
That you raised me to be.

47.

47. The First Time We Met

The first time I laid eyes on you
I couldn't help but stare.
Brand new, you captivated me,
Laid blissfully unaware.
Born only seconds earlier,
I gently scooped you up.
That moment we connected
And my heart was filled with love.

48.

48.   What Would I Do Without You

If you were not in my life, I do not know what I'd do.
I expect I would be searching for someone just like you.
I expect that I'd be looking for somebody to adore.
So it's lucky that I found the one my heart was waiting for.

In fact it was not lucky, it's just how it's meant to be
Because baby I've got you, and you know that you've got me.
That is how it's going to stay for the rest of our living days;
The way I feel when I'm with you, I want to feel always.

If you were not in my life, the skies would be grey
And I'd miss just being with you, every day.
I'd miss holding your hand and feeling so close;
I love so much about you, I don't what I'd miss most.

So what would I do without you? If I were all alone?
I'd definitely be without the greatest love I've ever known.
And I would be despondent, and miserable without a doubt.
So what I would do without you, is something I never will find out.

49.

49. Nomads' Land

It was a popular tourist spot
that people liked to visit;
they were drawn to its quirks
and all the things in it.
They pitched tents and wandered.
They explored every part,
carved their names into tree trunks
and took the place to their heart.
The high season was busy
before they left, one by one.
The streets soon became empty
With everybody gone.
Investing in property
they'd never sought to do.
With no intention of staying,
they were only passing through.

50.

50. Lost

She set out with intention;
Thought she knew the way to go
But as she wandered clumsily
The winds of change did blow.
They took her like a feather
And she floated on their breeze,
Soaring so far above the forest
She could barely see the trees.
At first, she was astounded
Just how far she went each day
But eventually she realised
She'd completely lost her way.

51.

51. Doodle

I took my pen.
I drew you out.
I got you wrong.
I rubbed you out.
I honed my craft.
I tried again.
I failed with mice
And then with men,
And then with landscapes
Laced with trees.
Where others seemed to draw with ease
My lines were sloppy,
Colours weak;
Your essence greyed,
Left incomplete.

52.

52.   Time Does Not Heal

Time does not heal
And you may never
Be the same.
But each day that passes
Means you're surviving
Despite the pain.

53.

53. Strangers To Friends

Encouraged
To see strangers
As
Friends
A trip to the park ends with a
Grin.
It begins with a coy hello
And before you know it
You are running around together
Enjoying the simple pleasures
Of slides and swings.
Uninhibited laughter rings free.
If only we never lost those values
How sweet life would be.

54.

54. Lead The Way

Ever feel like you're drifting?
Like you're going off course?
Like your efforts are being hindered
By some malevolent force.

The harder you push,
The less it works out,
So going with the flow
Is the best bet, no doubt.

You can't always be master
But you can lead the way.
Keep doing what you're doing
And it will come right one day.

55.

55. Other Ways

She was ragged at the edges.
She'd seen much better days
But beauty isn't surface deep;
There are so many other ways.

56.

56. Gardener Wanted

Her whole life's been a battle.
Her face is hard as stone
But inside, there's a garden,
Just waiting to be sown.
She's looking for a gardener
To give it TLC
And to bring out all the colours
No-one ever gets to see.

57.

57. Fishing For Stars

What if the skies were oceans
And the ocean was the sky.
What if the land were flooded
And all earthly seas ran dry.
You might not find the answers
Though clues hint to who you are.
It's still worth going fishing
as you might just catch a star.

58.

58.   A Note To The Husband

A happy wife is a happy life
And to make it even brighter,
Remember, that while you might be right
Your wife will always be righter.

59.

59.   Own The Sky

Spread your wings.
It's time to fly.
Make the leap.
Own the sky.

60.

60. You Belong With Me

You belong with me, my love
And I belong with you.
We should live life side-by-side
In everything we do.

You belong with me today,
For now and ever more.
And I belong with you, my dear,
The one that I adore.

We were meant to be, I know;
It's written in the stars.
I love the way we are as one
And everything you are.

Just think of all the moments
Aligning for us to meet.
So once we found each other
We were bound to feel complete.

But this part of our story
We'll sit and write together.
Hanging memories on the wall
Of the home we'll share forever.

So, both of us are certain
As we each say 'I do'
That you belong with me, my love,
And I belong with you.

61.

61. We Begin

We begin not by wanting to exist,
but by chance.
A complex dance of nature.
Nurtured. Take your
talk of fate and seek to make
more of your turn.
Learn what makes you tick
because you don't have to stick
with what is presented;
pretending it's your thing when it's not.
You've got the power and it's within you.
So begin.
Win your own definition of success
and don't settle for less, as giving up
only means you ensure that it will never happen.
Break the pattern.
If chance brought you here, you have nothing to fear
by beginning.
So take a chance, and never stop swimming.
By wanting not just to exist, we begin.

62.

62. Soul Of A Storm

She has the soul of a storm and the freedom of the wind.
She has eyes like the stars with moonshine within.
With the strength of the sea and lightning in her toes,
She dances on the breeze of change wherever she goes.
Hotter than a volcano and deeper than the oceans,
A whirling, swirling myriad of feelings & emotions.
She is daughter of the earth, primordially inspired.
She is water, she is wood. She is earth. She is fire!

63.

63. Hope

Hope is the place where you want to go.
Hope is the person who you want to know.
Hope is the feeling that carries you through
And hope is the future for me and for you.

64.

64. Showing You My Love

We are brought up to believe that love is something you feel
but to experience true love, you need to be shown that it's real.
You can hold love in your heart, though you can't hold it in your hand
And it takes somebody using their actions for you to truly understand.
Love lies in caring for another, to make their smile your world.
Love does not discriminate; it touches boys and girls.
It can make a grown man weep. It can make a woman strong.
Love can make you feel at home and it can make you feel you belong.
It's not just the massive gestures, sometimes small things are enough.
Just being there for somebody can make them feel your love.
It's not a scientific equation. It's not cultivated or grown.
But for certain, love can be visible, if only it is shown.

65.

65. Poison Pen Letter

Her pen was clearly poisoned;
despite her form and flair
as she tried to write the light
all that came out was despair.
She twisted words and syllables.
She played with rhyme and timing.
She ached to see the sunshine
after endless, fruitless mining.
So she said she'd stop her writing
as she couldn't feel the good
and each inky trope she wrote
was like letting her own blood.
She put her pen down somewhere
to save herself the pain
but the darkness, still consuming,
pulsed pervasive through her veins.
Whilst she tried to face the demons
who were dancing in her head
she revisited her pages,
highlighting all mistakes in red.
for this was her diary,
never intended for anyone else.
Her inkwell was her fear;
she had been poisoning herself.

66.

66. Am I Normal?

When asking if you're normal
The one thing you ought to know
Is all of us are struggling;
Some just never let it show.

67.

67.   Regret Or Repair

In moments of realization
You have a choice to make;
Either let regret consume you
Or rectify your mistake.

68.

68. Never Forgotten

I think of things you used to say
And all that you would do.
At some point, every single day,
My thoughts will turn to you.
To lose you was a bitter wrench,
The pain cut to my core.
I cried until my tears ran out
And then I cried some more.
This wouldn't be your wish for me,
That I'd be ever sad
So I try to remind myself
Of happy times we had.
I know I can't be with you now
And you can't be with me
But safe inside my heart you'll stay;
That's where you'll always be.

69.

69. Mirror Mirror

Mirror, mirror on the wall,
I don't think you know me at all.
Whilst you reflect the layer you see
Please realise there is more to me.
You cannot hope that frame and skin
Will let you read what lies within.
I'm fire and passion, soul and art,
Untamed spirit, giving heart.
And maybe beauty isn't mine
(I do not match the term defined)
But flesh alone will not speak for me;
I'm a book, come read my story.

70.

70.   Undefeated

She was tired and frustrated
But her task was uncompleted
So she carried on going
As she wouldn't be defeated.

71.

71. Brimful of Aspiration

Brimful of aspiration,
Of energy and passion,
She decided she was worth it;
That's when the magic happened.

72.

72.   Dare To Self-Care

Speak kindly to your inner self,
Don't take your demons' view.
You are you, and no-one else
Will lead the life you do.
Kill your inner critic
And silence all his chatter.
Then write this truth inside your brain;
"I'm worth it & I matter."

73.

73.   Out Of Our Hands

The world prizes possession
As a yardstick of success,
Adulating those with plenty
And berating those with less.
But perhaps this view is folly
And what sets us apart
Is not the things we own
But those we hold in our hearts.

74.

74.   The Universe Got Your Back

There's a myriad of voices
That are swirling in your mind,
Judging all your choices,
Questioning how you spend your time
And while society conditions us
To live a certain way,
The world is not that black & white;
There are many shades of grey.
You can have a go at anything
If you set your mind to it.
You don't need to ask the cosmos;
Just decide, and then pursue it.
Though if you listen carefully
When you're on the right track
You might hear the universe whisper
"Go get it! I got your back."

75.

75. Starmaker

The starmaker paused on the cusp of the day.
She straightened the sky; sent the sun on her way.
She welcomed the moon and he tipped her his grin.
Only once he was settled then she could begin.
With great sweeping motions and a flick of her wrist,
Her eyes truly sparkled as stars came to exist.
She twirled and she twisted until she was spent,
Leaving a sprinkle of glitter wherever she went.

76.

76.   Happy Memories

Life is too short to wake up with regrets.
Cherish the good times, the people you met.
The lessons they taught you,
The things you have seen,
Relish the memories;
The places you've been.
Think of the laughter,
Think of the sun.
Bask in the warmth of things you have done.
Your life and your choices,
The decisions you made,
Find joy each one
And smile as they're replayed.

77.

77. Let Love Shout Loudest

Let love shout loudest.
Let it surround us and consume.
Let it lift the heaviest hearts.
Let it brighten the darkest room
And as love breeds into infinity,
Let it bask in sun and moon.
May love weather every storm that breaks,
Enduring through the gloom.
Let love fortify the aged.
Let us teach it to our young.
Let love unite generations
And be passed to those to come.
Let love not be legend.
Let it be the way we live.
Let love be the gift;
We are ALL hardwired to give.
Let love build our cities.
Let love be our law.
Let love be the answer
To all knocks at the door.
Love tenderly, wholeheartedly;
Let it float upon the breeze.
Let it ripple lakes and waterways
And rustle through the trees.
Let love permeate the soil.
Let love pave the streets.
Let love be a home for all.
Let love be our heart beat.
Love passionately, love purely,
With purpose, without condition.
When the world is blinded
Let love restore its vision.

Let love be the question and also the reply.
May love not be disheartened, no matter who may try.
Let love be a comfort for the broken and weak.
Let love be the language that every soul speaks.
Let love be the melody that our spirits sing.
Let us live love.
Let love be the thing.

Thank you for reading!

Printed in Great Britain
by Amazon